Diminutive Voices, Volume 2: E–L

Diminutive Voices, Volume 2: E–L

Aphorisms, Epigrams, and Adages

KEN BAZYN

RESOURCE *Publications* · Eugene, Oregon

DIMINUTIVE VOICES, VOLUME 2: E–L
Aphorisms, Epigrams, and Adages

Resource Publications
An Imprint of Wipf and Stock Publishers
199 W. 8th Ave., Suite 3
Eugene, OR 97401

www.wipfandstock.com

PAPERBACK ISBN: 979-8-3852-4127-9
HARDCOVER ISBN: 979-8-3852-4128-6
EBOOK ISBN: 979-8-3852-4129-3
04/02/25

Contents

Acknowledgments

Once more I am pleased to thank Wipf & Stock for publishing so many significant books on a wide range of subjects and topics for a religious audience. Jonathan H. has creatively handled the typesetting and formatting, while Rockbrook Camera in Omaha has turned my 35mm slides into a beautiful CD.

Mention must also be made of my wife, Barbara, who has scrutinized every line for possible improvement. Finally, Brittany McComb has thoughtfully evaluated the grammar, meaning, and clarity, always keeping you, the reader, in mind.

Diminutive Voices

THE ECCLESIASTICAL CIRCUS

The kingdom of heaven is like a menagerie
of metaphysical jugglers, pastor-buffoons,
and newly-baptized freaks.

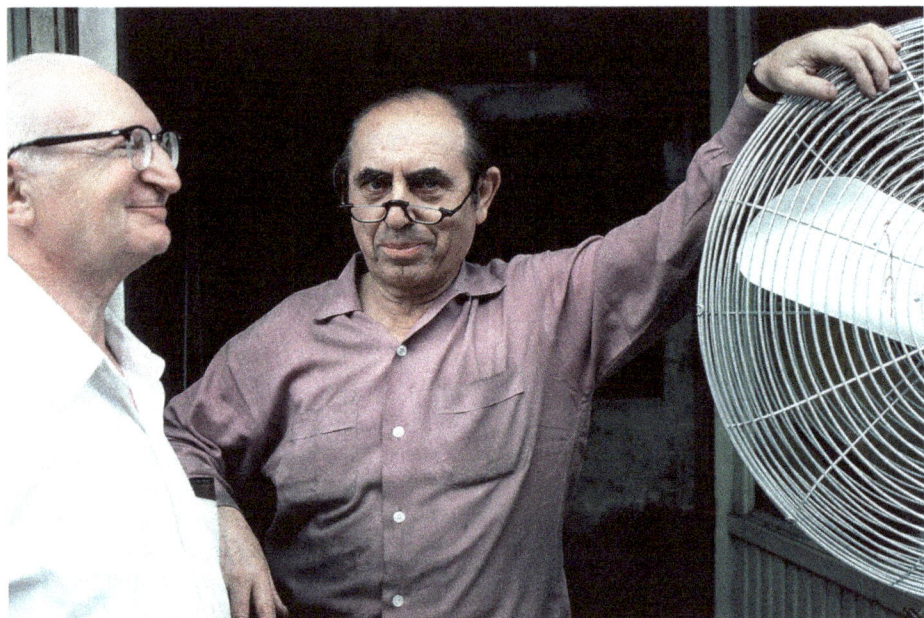

EH?

What did you say? Huh?
my auditory canal is filled with cloying puffballs.

ELOPEMENT ACCORDING TO HOYLE

The one-eyed jack of spades
has run off with the staid, prim diamond queen.

ELUSIVE PREY

Lepidopterist Montgomery
chasing after ghost satyr Rommel
with an Allied "panzer" net.

ENTHUSIASM SPROUTS

The evangelical mushroom
thrives on the rotting corpse of arid rationalism.

EROS

Gasping, inflatable buttocks
where a cartilage iota lengthens
to merge with its separate,
ecstatic dot.

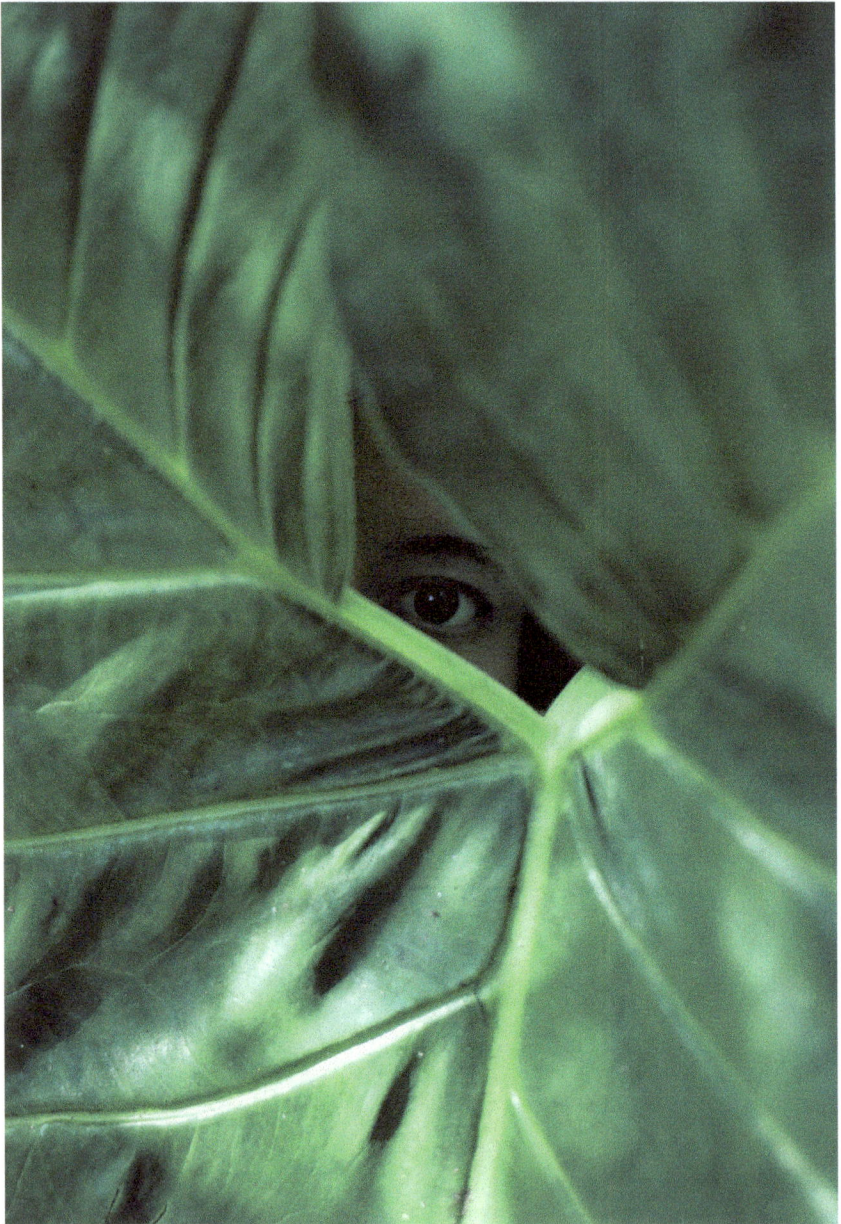

ETYMOLOGICAL QUAGMIRE

Expanding concentric circles of definition,
few any longer take aim at the bull's eye.

EVER HEAR OF ME?

Anonymity encloses me
in its gross, forgetful arms
tighter than my mother's elbows.

EXERCISING CAUTION

Disturb not sleeping dragons
for their first instinct is to slay.

THE EXHIBITIONIST

An elderly Casanova
whose erections only serve
to shock, disgust, and humiliate.

THE EXODUS

"430" years the Lord sees but waits,
then in the haste of one unleavened night
he pours out his firstborn wrath,
shoves murmuring Israel into wilderness freedom.

FIRE-EATER

The salamander in his charnel element
lapping up the candied flames.

FLICKERING HOPE

The Kingdom of Heaven is like a dimly-lit road sign pointing toward family reunion.

FLUTTER-FLIRTING

The eye enlarged by mascara
flaps coquettishly as foraging Lepidoptera.

FOR EMILY DICKINSON

The continent of possibility
is encircled by an ocean
of unbridled, outrageous fancy.

FORGETTING TO DECLAW

Making light of Samson,
gouging out his eyes,
but not clipping back his claws.

A FRANCISCAN FRIAR

I cast my lot
with the poor and wayward sheep
where the grass was scorched
and the water polluted by big industry upriver.

FUTILE FRIVOLITY

The cat unravels the basket of yarn,
chasing frizzy balls to their linear, disconcerting end.

THE GARDEN KING

In the garden court
the sunflower reigns supreme.

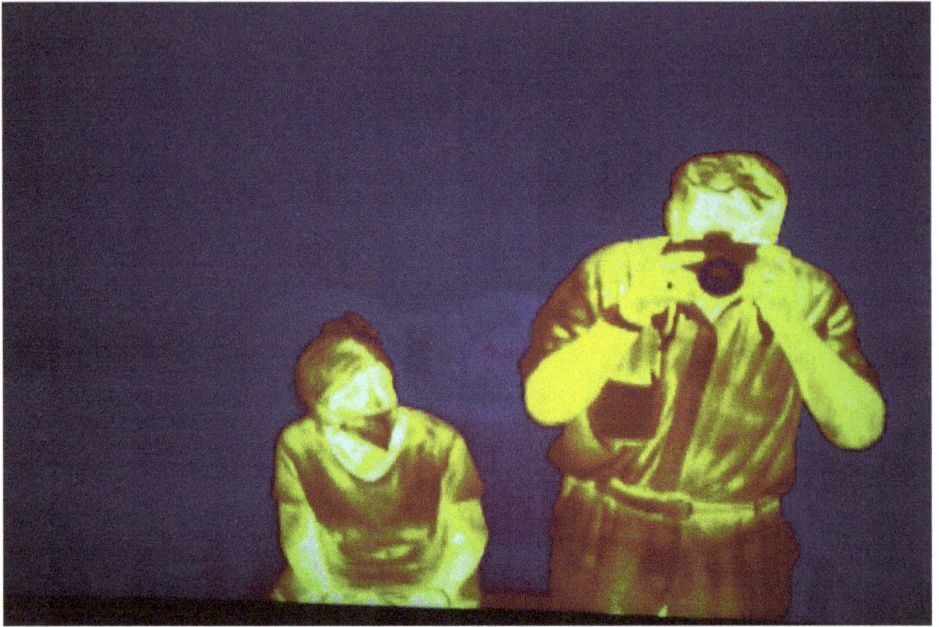

GENDER DIFFERENCES?

All I ever think about is sex, sex, sex:
how will each woman I see perform in the bed?
a woman has a broader, more wholesome perspective:
a man—how does he hug, kiss, and caress?

G. K. CHESTERTON, THE APOLOGIST

Bold as a righteous lion,
loud as a redeemed jackal.

GNAWING, INSIDIOUS INCURSIONS

I watch the barbarians like termites
chew the empire's edges.

A GOTHAMITE

Climbing a tree
to catch a perch,
my half-baked friend?

HANDS DOWN

I'll always prefer gray follicles
to chartreuse wigs.

A HEALING FAITH

In the crowds many hoped to be healed,
but only those who kept calling out, humiliating themselves,
tearing at the fringe of his garment,
drew out his full recuperative powers.

HEAVENLY ASPIRATIONS?

If Jesus is not your friend here,
why should you want to live with him forever?
Like attracts like. No one is comfortable with a stranger.

HILARIOUS ILLUSIONS

In the funhouse
whose figure isn't distorted
beyond recognition?

THE HOLY UNPREDICTABLE

Suppose God's not a continental gentleman,
will you hold your nose and walk on by?
Perchance God's not an eremitic fool, reeking with dung,
but wears a plaid suburban tie.
What if his love devours his friends
and it turns out hell is real?

HOMER: WHY SO LONG?

It's a stone's throw from Troy to Ithaca,
yet it took never-at-a-loss Odysseus
ten harrowing, dactylic years?

HOMILETIC PRELIMINARIES

How shall I preach
unless I have a definitive, critical text,
a pertinent, compelling topic,
and oh, my gosh! uproarious illustrations?

HORMONAL ATTRACTION

A hind follows after her leaping buck,
a ewe nuzzles her bellowing ram.

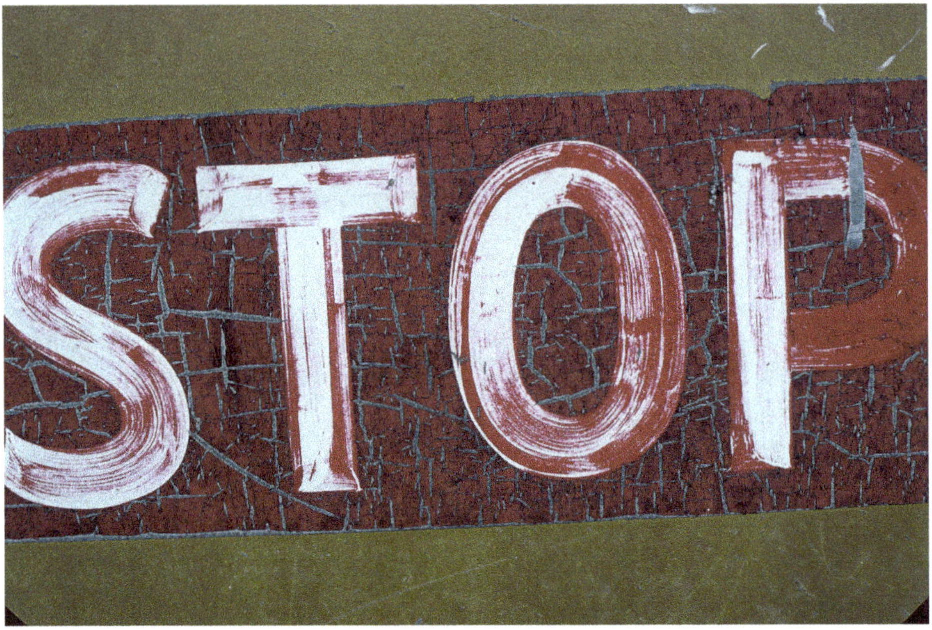
STOP

ILLITERACY

To the unlettered
the alphabet itself is
a mystic hieroglyph.

IMMUTABILITY

The earth opened up
and Korah rebelled against Beelzebul's leadership.

IMPURITIES

Crystals expel impurities,
while lugubrious cubes accumulate them like basest lead.

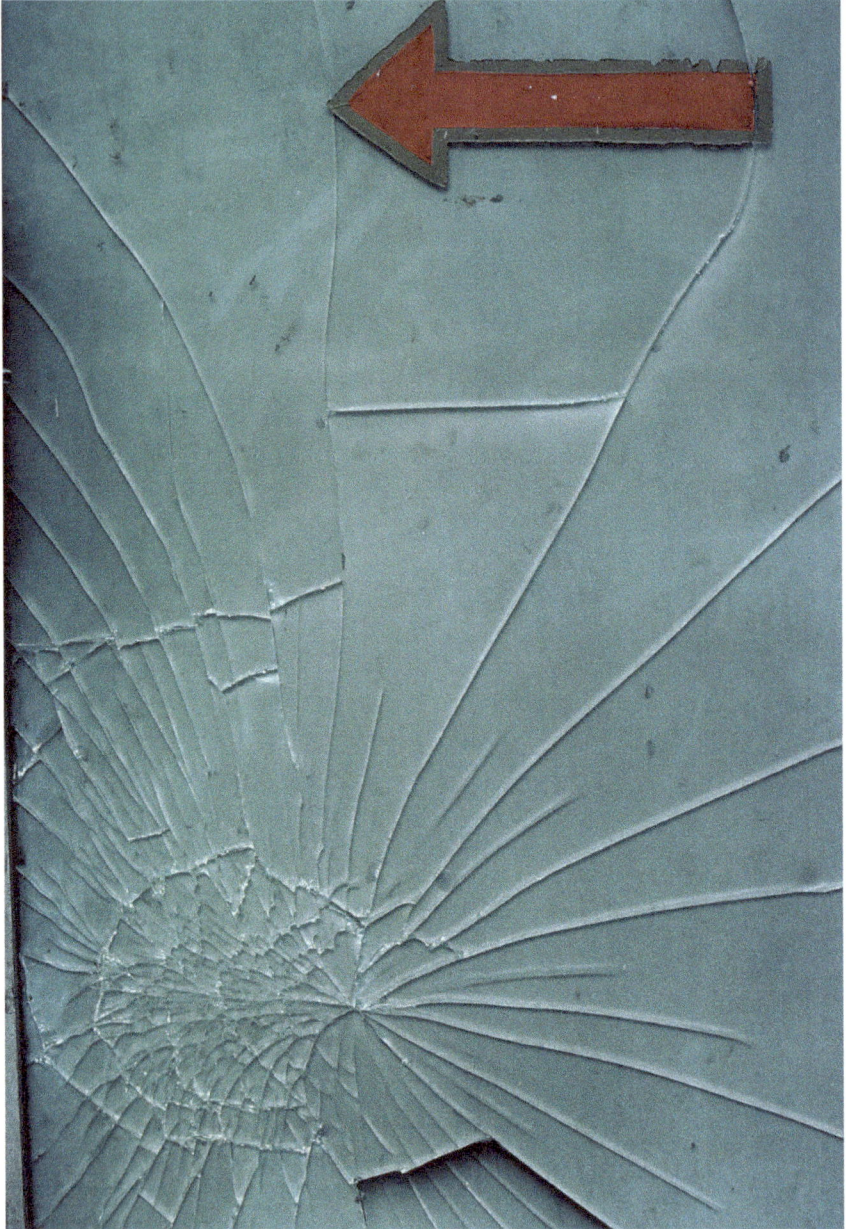

IN REVOLUTIONARY TIMES

Poison ran down the walls,
switchblades jeered from the streets,
a firebomb flew up like a sparkler.

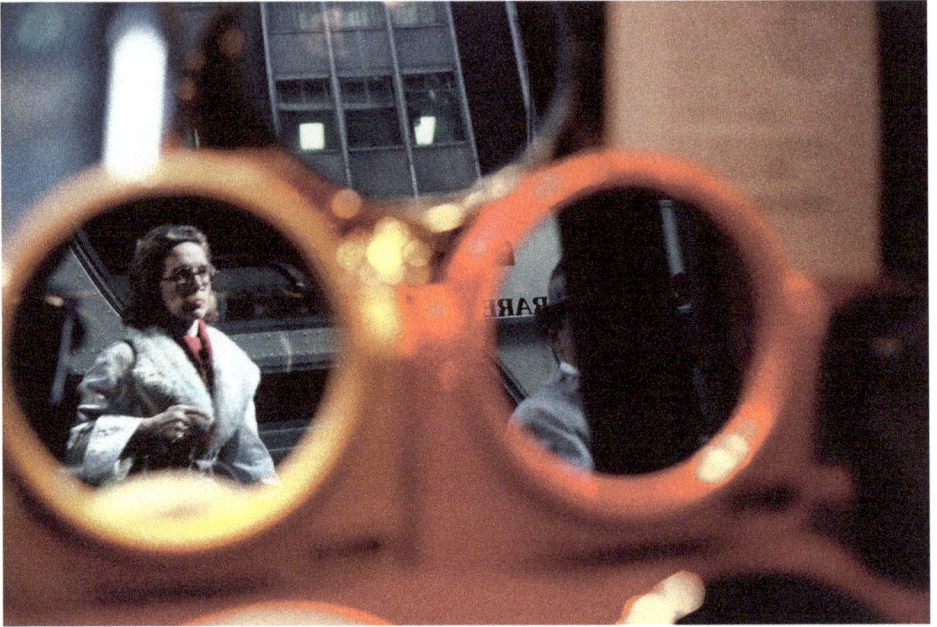

AN INCARCERABLE OFFENSE?

Stolen affections
embraced with anarchist infatuation.

INDELICATE CHOICES?

Do you prefer smooth breasts
or downy, long-legged ostriches?

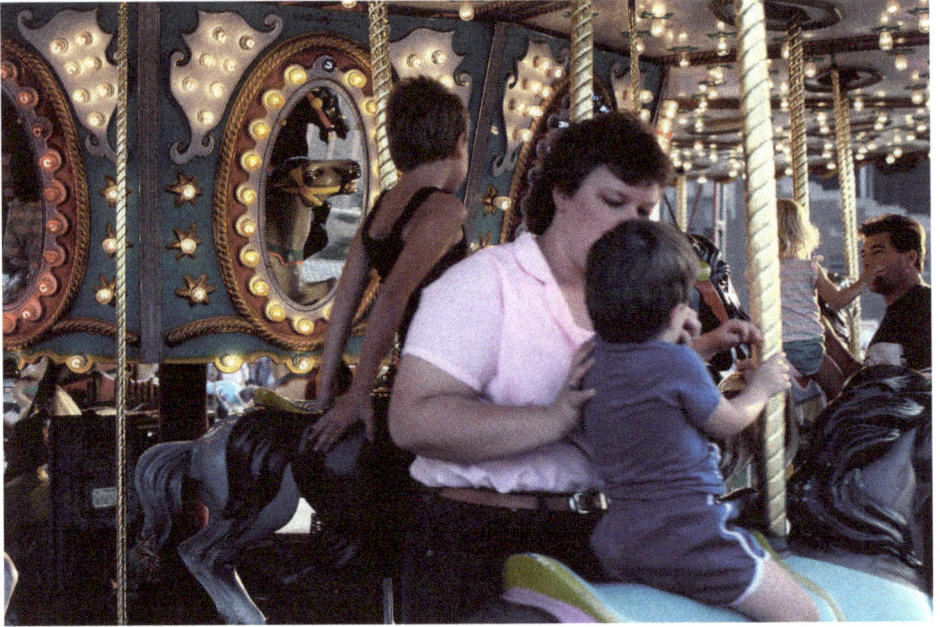

INFERIOR OFFSPRING

Is the Johnny-come-lately
ever superior to the original parent stalk?

INFIGHTING

Even Bohemians are rent asunder
by intolerant cliques and clans.

INNUENDO

The valet has the key
to my croissant lock.

INSUFFERABLE NECKTIES

Three people hang themselves every day
with their own insufferable neckties.*
                    —National Bureau of Statistics

---

* Editorial note: After the first month or so, this must seem a bit melodramatic.

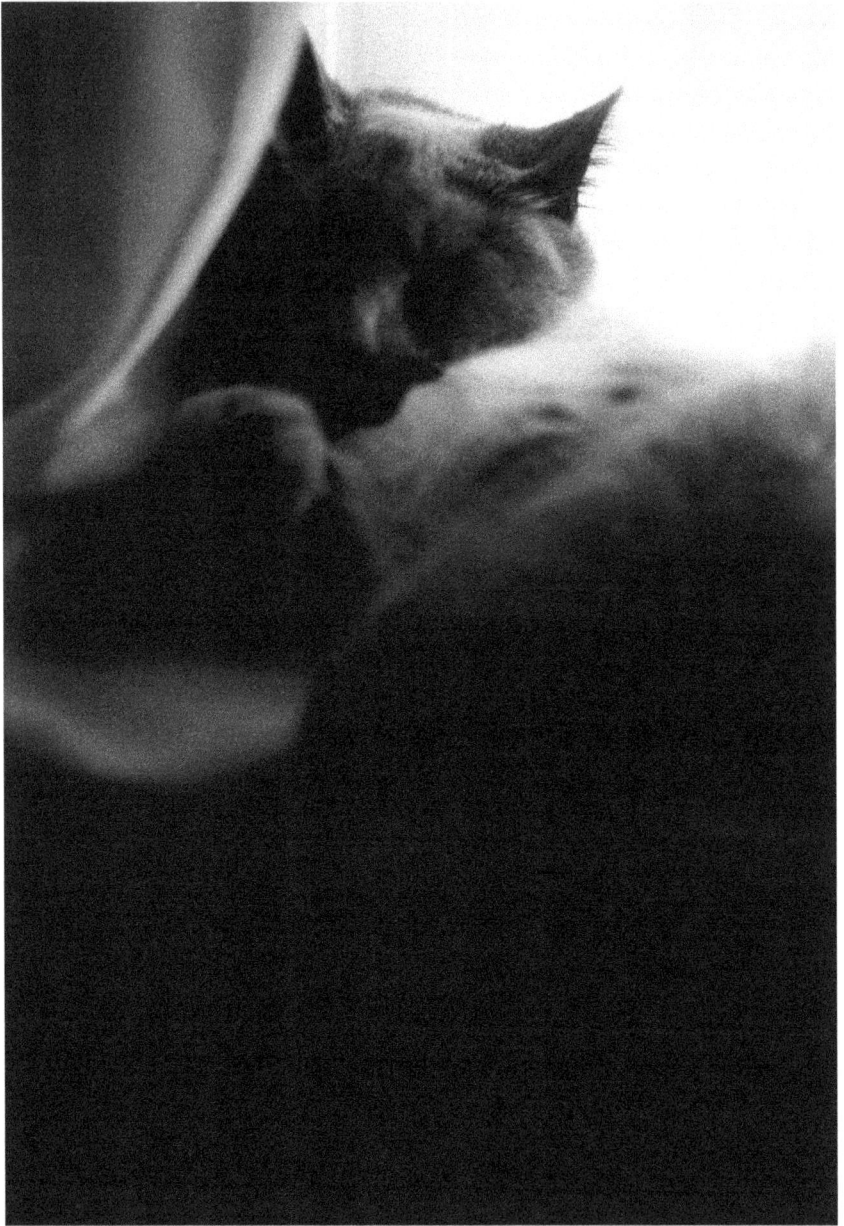

INVITING?

The inlaid, tempting grapes
high above pink Pompeii's
black lava couch.

LACK OF CLOSURE

A task as impossible
as slaying the nine-headed Hydra,
renewable where it bleeds.

LEFTOVER MIRACLES:
WHAT ANDREW SHOULD HAVE SAID

We've twelve baskets of crumbs, Jesus,
enough to feed a second multitude.

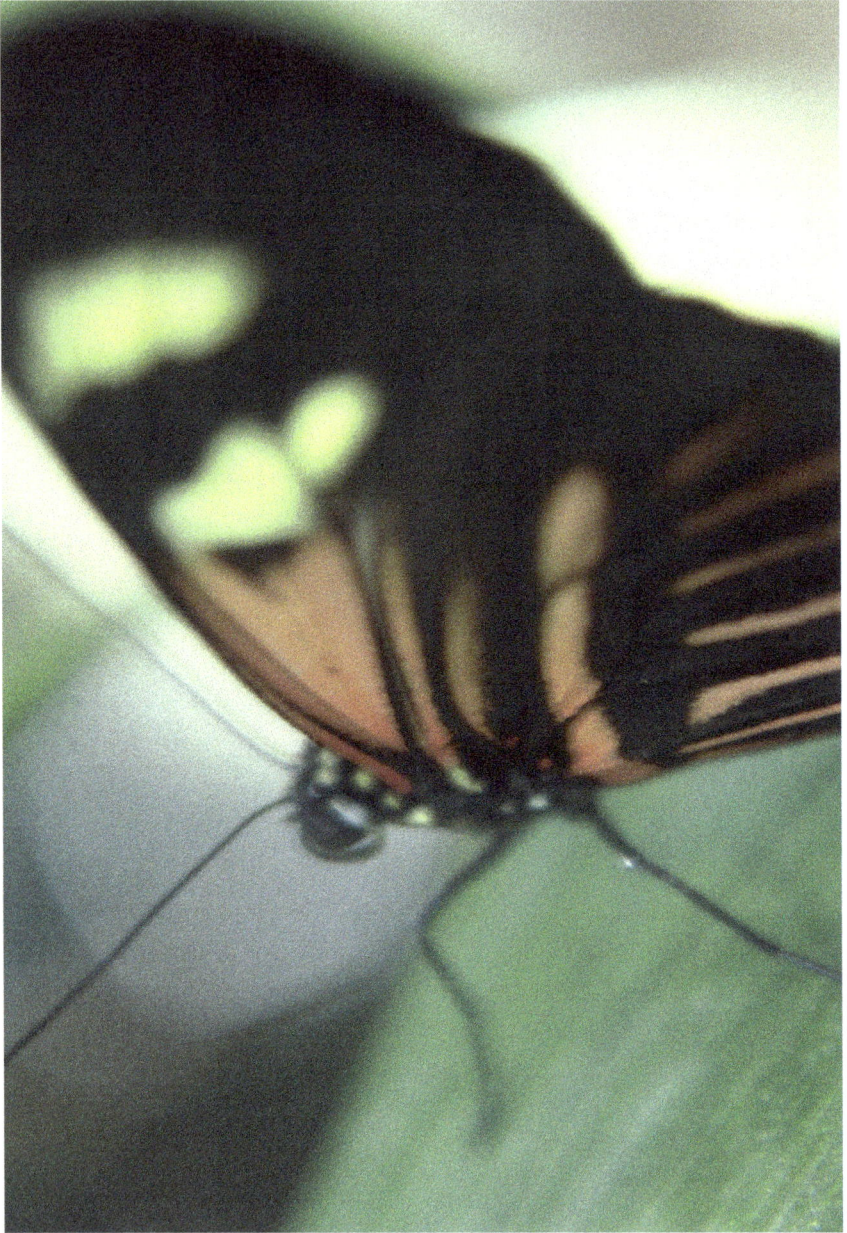

LEPIDOPTERA-MANIA

Painted Lady with a broken wing,
Monarch with a tarnished crown,
what am I
—but a lovelorn Swallowtail?

LIGHT VS. DARKNESS

The darkness is old, feeble, decrepit,
the light is young, brave, and handsome-strong.

LIKE OLD TIMES

I'll kiss your lipstick-smeared glass,
red with old Falernian.

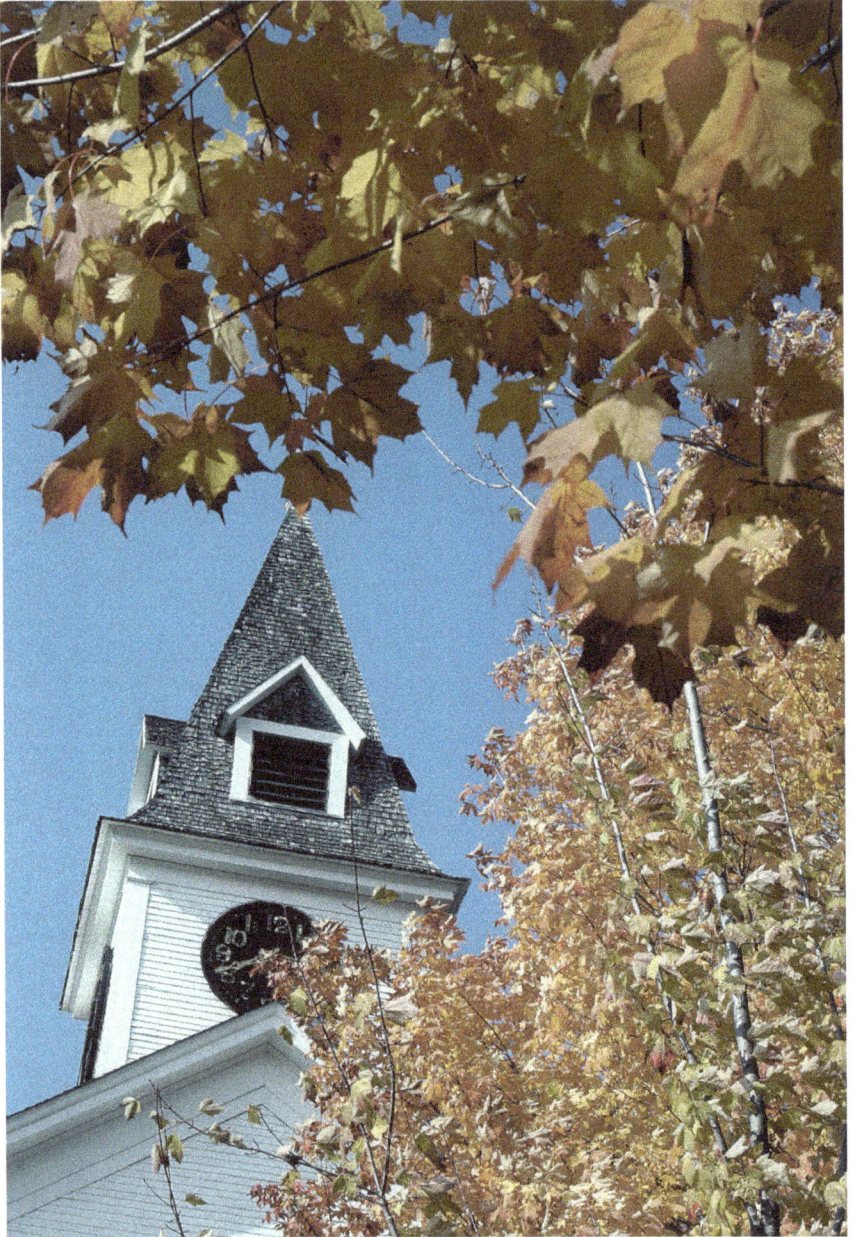

LOOKING HEAVENWARD

A steeple like a clapboard finger
pointing to the abode of God.

LOSING HIS DISTINCTIVENESS

Jesus, one of the minor saints
worshipped in the recesses of the side chapel of the cathedral,
deserving the orange curlicue candles.

Listing of Photographs

70. close-up of a kitten's face [Futile Frivolity]

71. close-up of sunflower [The Garden King]

72. man and woman on screen, Kiewit Luminarium, Omaha [Gender Differences?]

73. lion at zoo [G. K. Chesterton, the Apologist]

74. bitten and spotted leaf [Gnawing, Insidious Incursions]

75. street mural in Dubuque, Iowa [A Gothamite]

76. Jane and Henry Hatfield [Hands Down]

77. blind person and seeing-eye dog, Times Square [A Healing Faith]

78. cemetery, St. Francis de Xavier Catholic Church, Tucson, Arizona (yellow filter) [Heavenly Aspirations?]

79. girl making face in mirror [Hilarious Illusions]

80. portrait medallion of Alexander von Humboldt, Brooklyn Museum [The Holy Unpredictable]

81. boat at Chance Harbour, New Brunswick [Homer: Why So Long?]

82. adobe church, New Mexico [Homiletic Preliminaries]

83. dairy cattle near Peacham, Vermont [Hormonal Attraction]

84. painted stop sign [Illiteracy]

85. reflection at High Falls Gorge, Wilmington, New York [Immutability]

86. stone wall at Porter House Museum in Decorah, Iowa [Impurities]

87. arrow and cracked glass [In Revolutionary Times]

88. reflection in orange glasses of a woman and half of a man's face [An Incarcerable Offense?]

89. man sleeping on beach, woman in swimming suit [Indelicate Choices?]

90. mother and father with children on carousel [Inferior Offspring]

91. wig shop at 31st Street and 6th Avenue, Manhattan [Infighting]

92. female manikin legs and hand [Innuendo]

93. men in suits seen through truck window [Insufferable Neckties]

94. black cat sleeping [Inviting?]